A Note to My Black Daughter

by Toya L. Adams Driscal, MEd.

Illustrations by Rodney Potts
Cover Illustrations by Jessica Stevenson

Printed in the United States of America

ISBN 978-1-7358217-3-3

Ebook ISBN 978-1-7358217-4-0

First Printing, 2021

Toya L. Adams-Driscal, MEd.

www.toyaadamsdriscal.com

Cover Design by Jessica Stevenson

www.jlstevens19.myportfolio.com

Illustrated by R. Potts

RecollectionArt

Black Mom & Infant Daughter

Illustration By: Rodney Potts

To All the Black Moms who contributed to this project: THANK YOU from the depths of my heart and soul. This could have never been possible without you and your loving words of wisdom to not only your Black Daughter but to EVERY Black Daughter who might read these encouraging, inspiriting, loving words. May God continue to richly bless you and your Black Daughters!

Sincerely,

Toya Adams-Driscal, Med.

This book is dedicated to all the Black Daughters of the world

In loving memory of Marjorie Adams, a Black Daughter affectionately known to me as Granny & Bonnie Jean Adams, a Black Daughter affectionately known to me as Mommy

Foreword

A Mother's love is impenetrable, undeniable, and unmistaken. The Black Daughter is a commodity that needs to be treasured, nurtured, respected, esteemed and above all protected.

The term Kairos means a propitious moment for decision or action. Kairos in the Bible is a time that requires a conversion from people. Romans 13:11-13. A transition or transformation- a change of life. As our Daughters' transition through many stages of life it is important that they explore the world, tackle their fears, and try new things for God assists in discerning the Kairos.

The great poet Ralph Waldo Emerson said: "To be yourself in a world that is constantly trying to make you something else is the greatest accomplishment."

"A Note to My Black Daughter…" is an embodiment of expressive ways to teach, guide and love our young Black female descendants. Too many times our Black Daughters see images of themselves manufactured by others and that is why it is so imperative through their journeys that a Mother's love and wisdom is steadfast and unwavering.

Acknowledgment of Contributing Black Moms

Akiree Graves-Johnson

Amber Dumas

Andratesha Fritzgerald

Angie Oglesby

April Buckhanon

Aubrei Erkins

Brianna Riley

Carnesha Bates

Cathy Eddie

Cierra Driscoll

Courtney Bean-Jones

Danielle Birch

Dominica Drake

Donisha Bailey

Donnetta Gamble

Dyani Ellerb

Ernia Sims

Ethel L. Bodiford

Evette Clark

Felicia Douglas

Felicia Limage

Hollie Bodiford-Taylor

Jackie Massengale

Jennifer Threat

Kena Chappell

Kimberly Johnson

Maxine Peatross-White

Mendi Carrington

Michelle Norvell

Nicole Goode, Jacora's Mom

O'Dasha Blue

Ora D. Thomas

Pamela Smith

Pequita Hansberry

Ramona Hemmings

Goddezz Sadaqa Calhoun-Redus

Sherrell Britt-Turner

Sheryl Thomas-Washburn

Shiree Hildreth

Simone Brumfield

Stephanie Caldwell

Suzanna Coleman

Tracey Harrison-Coates

Tracy Reid

A Note to My Black (Bonus) Daughter Jamir...

I want to begin by saying I love you and how proud I am of you and ALL of your many AMAZING accomplishments. Although I am not your biological Mom, you have been a huge part of my life since you were 5 and it has been my pleasure to watch you grow into the Woman you have become thus far.

We have been through many ups and downs over the years but I want you to know and always remember: I love you and only want the absolute best for you in every aspect of your life. There have been many tears shed and prayers offered up for you over the years and I thank God for placing you (and your brother, Jalen) in my life at the right time. You taught me what parental love truly is; I gleaned so much from being your "step" Mom that helped me when I actually became Mason's Mom. I pray that you know and understand that everything came from a place of love in hopes that you would be better.

As a Black Woman in today's society, like myself and every other Black Woman, we are the most unprotected and abused group on the planet. We have always bore so much for everyone else, and while many might see that as something negative, honestly, that is what makes us so powerful; I want you to walk in that power and remember it when you are feeling inadequate. Walk in your calling (whatever that might be) and be unapologetically you at all times; never shrink to fit into someone else's opinions or molds of who they think you should be because you are so much greater than that.

Here are a few wisdom nuggets for you to remember as you continue on this journey called life:

❖ *Failure is a necessary stepping stone to success.*
❖ *Always be you-never decrease or shrink because of others' insecurities about themselves.*
❖ *You are and will always be enough.*
❖ *"No one can make you feel inferior without your consent" –Eleanor Roosevelt*
❖ *Know, understand the importance of self-love and practice it often*
❖ *Learn to appreciate the gifts of knowledge your elders share with you.*
❖ *Love those in your life with not only words but deeds as well because they will not be here always and you do not want to live with the regrets of not showing it to them.*
❖ *Remember, "in all things we (YOU) are more than conquerors through Him who loved us" (Romans 8:37-NIV).*
❖ *Never burn a bridge that you may have to cross again.*

Continue to showcase your magnificence in the remarkable way that only you, Jamir Carolyn Huston, can do!

Love Always...Toya

A Note to My Black Daughter, To MY Beautiful Black Daughter, Halo, My Lo-Bot...

It has taken me months to figure out the perfect start to this letter. Then I realized this letter is like Motherhood, imperfectly perfect!

Halo, your seed was implanted with LOVE. You were prayed for. I pictured you well before you were created. The best part of being your Mother is watching your personality take form. At 20 months, you are courageous, you are an explorer, you are free. As you grow things will change, people will change. Opinions and views may be pushed on you. But always stay true to yourself and what you believe in. Do not allow anyone to stuff you into a box; myself included.

Beautiful Brown Girl, you are amazing.
Beautiful Brown Girl, you are worthy.
Beautiful Brown Girl, you are needed.
Beautiful Brown Girl, you are capable.
Beautiful Brown Girl, your hair is your crown.
Beautiful Brown Girl, your hair is beautiful and strong.
Beautiful Brown Girl, your hair is resilient.
Beautiful Brown Girl, you are fearless.
Beautiful Brown Girl eat the chips stacked against you.
Beautiful Brown Girl, friends are important, genuine friends.
Beautiful Brown Girl, love yourself first. Then love and be loved.
Beautiful Brown Girl chase your dreams.
Beautiful Brown Girl do not be afraid of restarting.
Beautiful Brown Girl, color outside the lines.
Beautiful Brown Girl, what is for you, will always be for you.
Beautiful Brown Girl, you are the heart and soul.
Beautiful Brown Girl pull up your own chair and table.
Beautiful Brown Girl, never break yourself into bite size pieces... Make them choke!

"The natural state of Motherhood is unselfishness. When you become a Mother, you are no longer the center of your own universe. You relinquish that position to your children." – Jessica Lane

My Lo-Bot, be better than I,
As I am better than my Matriarch,
As she is better than hers...

Love Always...Mommy

A Note to My Black Daughter, Punka...

One letter will never encapsulate all that I want to say to you, but this letter is unique for this moment in time for who I am and who you are becoming. My intention is that this letter grows with you, and resonates through Many seasons and situations. I am so thankful God saw fit for me to be your Mom, you are truly the BEST gift He has ever given me. There is never a dull moment with you-due to your thoughtfulness, awareness and quick witted sense of humor. I am stretched and challenged to be the best version of myself daily in order to be the best mother to you. I examine and learn from my missteps and parenting fails to learn what you need to thrive and be your best. Be intentional to make adjustments and give yourself grace. The goal in life is progress, not perfection.

Dearest Ari, take your enthusiasm, charisma, creativity and vibrancy and share it with the world! I know you are destined for greatness beyond what my imagination holds. Some may try to deter and discourage you, but remember, people's opinions are not who God says you are. The vision God gives you is yours. The fact that others cannot see your vision does not make it any less real or valid for you. Give yourself permission to go for what God has purposed for you and choose life every day. Keep dreaming. Keep smiling. Keep laughing. Keep dancing. Most importantly, keep close to God every step of the way. You make me so very proud and I love you!

Always Remember-Deuteronomy 30:19 (NIV) which says: "This day I call the heavens and the earth as witnesses against you that I have set before your life and death, blessings and curses. Now choose life, so that you and your children may live"

Love Always...Mom

A Note to My Black Daughter Ailani...

There is a freedom that you are stepping into as you fight to become the very best version of yourself. Every battle that you enter into - both the ones you talk about and the ones you never speak of have worth if they bring about your freedom. You are free to dream unlimited dreams, free to try unbounded endeavors, and free to live the life God has ordained for you.

Freedom to dream is space you may have to fight to occupy. My dearest Daughter, you do not have to have it all figured out. You do not have to know the formula or the pathway. Dreams open doors to worlds that others cannot even imagine until YOU DO! Take time to dream. Dare yourself to take the limitations off of your imagination and commit to receiving God's vision for the impossible to become reality. Your dreams will bring solutions that the world does not yet know it needs.

Freedom to try is a grace that only you can give to yourself. In that grace you create an environment that accepts the personal elemental bond of being both imperfect and content. There are questions that haunt those who chase perfection, that will never touch you. You are one who has learned that art is filled with failure turned into glory. You are free to try, learn, fall, learn, dig deep, learn and get up to learn some more. Trying gives you the experience to recognize triumph when you meet it.

Freedom to live is your birthright. The Bible says that Jesus came that we might have life and have it more abundantly. This is His promise to your heart. Live! Experience life. Take time to be present and enjoy each moment. Breathe in the miracles that life offers to you. Experience the fullness of the one life that is a gift from God to you.

You are Black, beautiful, brilliant and becoming more authentically you every single day. The moment you step onto a path that allows you to dream freely, try bountifully and live abundantly is the moment that you step into the zone where your greatness powers your next step. You are a gift to this world. My prayer is that you will see yourself as God sees you and love yourself as God loves you. I pray that you will dream, try, live in freedom now and forever. I love you! I am proud to be your Mommy. I have loved you from the Moment your existence was made known to me. I will love you for eternity.

Love Always...Mommy

Photo By: *Anita Louise Photography*

A Note to My Black Daughters Niki & Toni…

I love you both so very much…You are my world!

I could not write you individually as I feel the same and love you each equally, despite the little differences in you…so why write it twice? ▢

Niki & Toni, I am so honored to call you my Daughters!

Twice I have closed my eyes and in a single moment suddenly you each stood in front of me a Strong, Determined, Loving Black Woman, where my Cute Baby Girl once stood. You are each one of my Masterpieces! I have lost count of how many times you have said or done something and I said to myself "WOW…She got it!" I am so proud of both of you! I have always wanted the world and much more for you and I am constantly reminded that you are going for it!

Always keep that Spirit and that Fire in your Soul! Your Drive, Passion and Determination; stay focused on your worth, protect your energy and by all means…tell your story! Blow your own horns my Bright Stars! Continue to Believe in Yourself and Support One Another!

Always straighten your crowns when it tilts and remember if you need help, me and your sister are here to help you!

You all are too big for me to carry but know that you are always carried in my heart!!

You are a wonder Blessing…A Treasure from above
Your Laughter, Warmth and a special Charm…You are Beauty & Love
You bring a special joy from deep inside & fill my heart with pride
With every year that passes, you are more special than before!
No words can describe our memories, the pride and gratitude, too.
That comes from having Strong Black Daughters Just Like You!

Remember to share your love, strength, beliefs, determination, drive and support with your children and one day you will be overwhelmed with these wonderful feelings I have for you!

I Love You My Babies, My Black Queens!!

Love Always…Mommy

A Note to My Black Daughter Kennedy, My Honey Bun…

The day that you were born was one of the happiest days of my life. I am so grateful that God chose me to be your Mother and I do not take that responsibility for granted. As your Mother, I have been able to witness you grow into a beautiful young lady who loves to dance and has a passion for telling stories. Your intelligence and love for others shows in everything that you do. I am overjoyed that you have a sincere love for Christ and that you have chosen Him as your Savior. I love you Kennedy, you are a light in my life. I am so excited to see all the things that life has in store for you, and I know that you will let your light shine bright regardless of any challenges that you may face. Whatever path you choose in life, I hope that you keep God first and remember that your greatness is not determined by others. Kennedy you are a rare jewel that God has given me, and I am so proud to be your Mother.

Love you Always…Mom

A Note to My Black Daughters...

To My Jordyn,
You were my first baby, the first person to know the sound of my heartbeat from the inside. We had an unexplainable bond from the very first Moment I knew I was pregnant. When you were born, you never wanted to leave my side, and for six months you didn't. As exhausted as I was, I was thankful for every Moment. Every single day, I continue to be thankful for each and every Moment with you. God is so good! You are so observant, smart, loving, thoughtful and just a joy. Your laugh makes my heart smile. Continue to grow and shine my beautiful Girl. I love your face!

To My Ashlyn,
My baby, my grand finale! I knew I was pregnant with you before taking any tests. It was as if I could feel your marvelous spirit glowing inside of me. You have done it your way since you were in my womb, and I love that about you. I love your spunk, creativity, how caring you are, your honesty and your desire to learn and grow. It makes me so happy that you always want to be right up under me (even when I tell you to give me room). Continue to be bold and beautiful you my love! I love you Ash!

Love Always...Mommy

Photo By: McKinley Wiley – The Darkroom Company

A Note to My Black Daughter Alaya, My Sweet Pea…

I prayed for you…years prior to God blessing me with you. I prayed for you specifically my special little Girl. When I found out about you, I knew you would bless my life tremendously. I prayed for you. I Manifested you, my sweet baby, years before my dream came true. I prayed for you. You could not have come into my life at a better time although the world soon turned crazy following the great news of you growing inside of me. You gave me strength and reminded me to keep going during death and a global pandemic. You kept my hopes and spirit high when I wanted to just give up. You gave me confidence in the midst of confusion. You let me know I was strong and built to take on any obstacle that was placed in my face. You also kicked my butt in pregnancy but that is a different story to tell (lol). You came out a firecracker yet so beautiful and sweet. As years go by and you grow older and wiser, I want you to remember these words. Remember that you were prayed for. Remember that you are loved. Remember that God blessed this Earth with you because you are that damn special. Alaya, I want you to remember to keep your fire when the world tells you that you are too much. Remember that you are beautiful inside and out despite what the world may tell you. Remember that your skin beams like silk and glows like the finest piece of gold. Remember that your hair is of Goddesses and royalty. Remember you are strong even in weakness, my Girl. You are FIERCE baby! As we grow together on this Mother and Daughter journey, I hope we become best friends. I hope to be someone you look up to and share your secrets with. I hope to remain strong and demonstrate what a dope Mother is. I hope to leave you with so much knowledge about life and Womanhood. I know in my heart we got this! Remember you are and will forever be my unicorn, my Black Girl Magic, my baby Girl, the one I prayed for, Ms. Alaya Brittany Riley.

Love Always…Mommy

Photo By: Kenneth Farmer

A Note to My Black Daughter Kayla…

I want to say, I Love You So Much! You changed my life for the better. I will always want nothing but the best for you, you are very special to me. In my eyes, there is no one that can equal your beauty. I am proud of you. Remember to wear your crown proudly and only adjust it when needed.

Love always…Mommy yo' Girl!

A Note to My Black Daughters, Denise Nicole and Maya Sheree …

I never imagined to what extent my life would change once I became a mother. Unfortunately, my first pregnancy resulted in a miscarriage and I can recall the doctor asking me if I was okay and if I needed counseling? My immediate response was "No doctor, I am okay. I believe in the Lord and I will place all my trust and faith in Him." I continued to share with him that everything happens for a reason and I was not going to question why? Not long after and by the grace of God I became pregnant again. On June 27, 1990, Denise Nicole you entered the world and I became a Mother. You were perfect. You resembled a China doll with loads of Black hair. Now at age thirty, you remain loving, inquisitive, intelligent and career driven. You are a good listener, focused, dependable, organized, helpful and strive to accomplish nothing less than the best in every phase of your life.

On March 29, 1993, God blessed our family with another perfect baby Girl. Maya Sheree, you made a bold entrance into the world and reminded me of a little bumble bee, wrapped in a blanket and your head covered with a pink and purple striped cap. You were a happy baby with the cutest, bright smile. Now at age twenty-seven, you still remain small in stature, fierce, while displaying a calm, sensitive side. You are loving, caring, nurturing, and have a compassionate heart. You do not like confusion but choose to live peacefully while sharing an encouraging word. You have always been a hard worker and it is evident that you are dedicated to your career. You display much care and compassion for children of autism and those with disabilities.

What a privilege to be the mother of two beautiful, Black Women. Denise and Maya you are special because you were designed by God with your own unique talents and abilities. You are God fearing Women, growing in faith and spirit. You have witnessed Many positive and negative situations happening in the world around you. You have experienced that life can be beautiful, but also that life can be cruel and unfair. You have been raised to be strong Women and you know the importance of being treated with respect and dignity. Your support system is strong and your sisterly bond is inseparable. Though not perfect, you both continually strive for greatness in your daily walk, your careers, and in your faith. Now that you are engaged to the Men of your dreams, it brings much joy to see how happy you both are. More than you know I sit back and watch how you apply much love, kindness, affection, and positivity into your personal relationships and how it is returned to you. What more could a Mother ask for?

My prayer is that you always remember to be grateful for everything. With God by your side you can overcome all obstacles. He has given you abundant life and an everlasting life to come. Both of you have been graced with the ability to do good works, to love, share, encourage, and care for others around you. Hold strong to your faith and continually seek the Lord for guidance and strength. Most importantly thank Him and praise Him every day. I am so proud of the Women you have become, I thank God for you, and count it all joy to be your Mother.

Love Always…Mommy - Cathy Eddie

A Note to My Black Daughter Madison, My Sweet Girl...

I believe in you more than you can imagine. Just know you can be anything that your little heart desires but always remember to be yourself. Despite what you may face in this world, please remember to always be kind. Be brave enough to say what you want even if others do not agree. Never forgot how worthy you are. Your voice matters and so do you ~ You are ENOUGH!

Love Always...Mommy

A Note to My Black Daughter, Harper Monét, My Moni Love, My Pookie...

April 25, 1997 will forever be my favorite day...because it is the day that I gave birth to you...my firstborn child. You were the most beautiful, most precious and most perfect human I had ever laid eyes on. You taught me a whole new meaning of unconditional love. You were my personal baby doll and will forever be my baby no matter how old you are. This is why I call you my Baby Woman. ☺

Being the Mother of you and your brother is my most favorite role. I am so honored that God chose me to be your Mother. If I could pick from all of the little Girls in the world I would pick you every time! Mother-Daughter relationships can be tricky and you definitely kept me on my toes. I knew you were always watching and imitating me. I wanted you to know the importance of being respectful to others no matter their age or status. I wanted you to know how to speak up for yourself and to have self-love. I wanted you to be honest, classy, loving and caring. As parents, we pour into our children all of the life lessons we can possibly think of to ensure we are giving them the tools they need to be a successful member of society with sound morals and values. As I watch how you handle yourself and take care of business, I am more than pleased with what I see.

You are one of the brightest people I know and I love your care and compassion for others, especially the less fortunate. I am so proud of the young Woman you have become. You have organizational and leadership skills that are unparalleled. I have observed you putting your God given skills and talents to use throughout your life and I am always amazed at what I witness. The things I wanted for you as you were growing up have come full circle. When I said I wanted you to speak up for yourself you did and continue to do just that! I am reminded of your college graduation cap that said, "She likes to argue so I sent that Girl to law school"! That was the PERFECT statement! I know you are going to be an amazing attorney and I wait with great anticipation to see all of the Many accomplishments you will experience. I am and will always be your biggest fan and loudest cheerleader!

As a Black Woman I want you to always know that you are enough! Continue to love the skin you are in. Know your worth and never settle for anything less. Remember to speak and believe an affirmation you spoke as a young Girl...YOU ARE THE BADDEST WOMAN ON THE PLANET! And always remember...YOU ARE BRAVER THAN YOU BELIEVE, STRONGER THAN YOU SEEM, SMARTER THAN YOU THINK and LOVED MORE THAN YOU KNOW!

I love you with every ounce of my being, Pook! January 2021

Love Always...Mommi

Black Mom & Young Daughter

Illustration By: Rodney Potts

A Note to My Black Daughters, Jaelle & Jaia…

You were created in love and with love. On purpose and in purpose.

> *A gift of life. A present to this world to make an imprint.*

You are a Black Woman,

> *Your skin is rich like the soil of the Earth. Created to enrich and produce life. You are a diamond,*

> *Far more precious than rubies, created to make your way, you are virtuous. Keep kindness on your tongue and take care of yourself. Stand strong in wisdom and integrity. ~ Proverbs 31:10*

You are fearfully and wonderfully made by God in His likeness,

> *God is with you always; you shall not fear. For anything bound against you shall not prosper. ~ Psalms 139, Isaiah 54*

Follow your passions in spite of what others may say.

> *For the Lord knows the plans He has for you, plans to help and not hinder you to give you hope. ~ Jeremiah 29:11*

Love God and yourself first,
You are protected and respected by Him so do the same for yourself. Know your worth.

When you are feeling pressed, remember diamonds are made under pressure you are destined for greatness and to shine bright.

Be the most educated. Speak from the knowledge you obtain and seek. Knowledge is the one thing that can never be taken from you.

Be Phenomenal. Be authentic. Be transparent. Be you unapologetically. Take up space wherever you are and be a light and a voice in the face of adversity. Walk in purpose on purpose always.

You are a Black Woman. Beautiful and strong. You stand on the shoulders of all the great Black Women that have come before you. Be historic.

Nobody said life would be easy, but stay the course follow your passions and desires. Lean on God to guide your footsteps and understanding. Show and share your light in the world in all you do.

Love Always…Mommy Danielle M. Birch

A Note to My Black Daughters, To My Three Girls…

I am so proud of the young Women you are becoming. You are so different in every way but when I see the love and companionship the three of you share, I have tears in my eyes. You are proof that love has no color. The three of you are blessed to have your own beautiful shade of color coming from one Black Woman. I have always prayed that you all would love who you are, having self-worth and self-love so that you never feel less than, unworthy, or incapable of obtaining anything you put your mind to. I apologize for falling short in Many areas but I thank GOD, and pray to GOD daily for you.

Khrystian, you have always not allowed anything or anyone to rush you. I first said you were just slow. However, watching the decisions, you make, I have come to understand it is you understanding your worth. You will do things when they are right for you and not when someone else deems them necessary. I am in awe of your commitment to your truth.

Amirah, your pursuit of wisdom is to be applauded. Your maturity during stressful times provides a pace for your family that assists in them getting through. Your level of expectation for the things, treatment, education, finance and care applied to your being is a characteristic that I love about you, I am in awe of your commitment to your truth.

Laila, your determination to get things right will allow you to have an expectation of excellence but learning to laugh at yourself, not take things so seriously, and attempt to understand others point of view gives me hope that you will show empathy, compassion, and love for all. Your growth shows me that you are on a path to understanding and acceptance. You know who you are at this Moment but you know that you will grow into an even more beautiful creation of GOD. I am in awe of your commitment to your truth.

Girls my prayer, desire, and hope for you is that you KNOW the gift of GOD that you are to Mommy, this world and the universe. I pray that you will seek wisdom, you will be compassionate, moral, honest, loving, forgiving and most of all that you will pursue a personal relationship with Christ. This world has relied on the shoulders of Black Women to hold it up. We provide love, care, inspiration, help, and finances for our children, others' children, spouses, bosses and coworkers. We are often not acknowledged, and overlooked for the contributions provided. However, KNOW that the people of this world come from your powerful DNA.

Mommy loves you for life.

Love Always…Mommy

A Note to My Black Daughter, Anya Marie, My Little Nugget...

From the Moment that you entered into this world I knew that you were a beautiful, brave, special, amazing, little Black Girl that would one day grow into a strong, determined, loving, and successful Black Woman. I knew that this world would test you, try to defeat you, and try to hinder your success. I knew that you were going to have to fight twice as hard to accomplish your goals in life because you were Black and a Girl.

I also knew that you had Black Girl Magic inside of you that could never be taken from you. Use that magic to strive and dream for whatever makes you happy! Hold on to it always, and never let it go! I want you to know and understand all the beauty that is you, inside and out. I want you to know your worth, and know that whatever you set your mind to you can do it!

You can not only dream, but you can actually become...a doctor, an entrepreneur, an author, President of the United States, all of the above, or something completely different. You can be whatever your heart desires as long as you are determined to do so. Sky's the limit is an understatement. Universe is the limit!

Love Always...Mommy

A Note to My Black Daughter, Syrenity, My Love…

I never knew what love meant until I birthed you. Before you, I was in a dark headspace in my life. I did not feel loved or even validated. The day that I became your Mom, I knew that my life would change, but at that time I did not know how. You have brought me nothing but joy and light even in the times when I have to redirect your decisions. The day that I became your Mom is the day that you saved me. You saved me from living an immature life to now being a responsible adult that is responsible for another human being. God does not miss and when I think of you and look at you, I am blessed that He was right on target. You have blessed me in so Many ways.

You are creative, loving, smart, genuine, and kind. You have so Many qualities about you that I admire. I know that when you enter into adulthood, you will be a leader. People will embrace you and cling to you because of the unique boldness that you are already starting to show at the ripe age of 9 years old. The most recent role that I admire about you is "Big Sister"; you are very attentive to Jacoby's needs. When he cries, you answer right away. I admire your attentiveness to even the smallest details of brushing his hair. I am beyond grateful to God that he sent such an amazing Daughter such as you. I want you to know that you can do whatever you put your mind to. You are not limited in the possibilities that are available to you. Our Madame Vice President, Kamala Harris is an example of the endless possibilities you have available to you. Do not EVER let anyone tell you that you cannot do anything. If you think about it and are passionate about it, then the next step is to just step out on faith and do it. I love you and I pray nothing but blessings over your life.

Love Always…Mommy

A Note to My Black Daughter D'yari aka Mama Girl . . .

This letter is to my other half the prettiest Girl in the world! I thank God every day for blessing me with a mini me. You were brought into my life at the right time. Mommy was scared when she found out about you, but I knew I could not let you down. From feeling your slight movements turn into big movements, your tiny kicks turn into big kicks, and watching you grow so big and healthy in Mommy's tummy I knew God made me invincible and capable to be the best mommy I could be for you. I love how independent and brave you are to do new things. I love how you look at me to insure that whatever you are getting into is safe! You are my safe haven; Mommy would not know what to do without you. I just hope that I am doing this Mommy thing right and raising you to be the best Woman that this world has ever seen! I will always be here for you and support you from your littlest accomplishments to the biggest of all.

A Note to My Black Unborn Daughter. . .

Mommy loves you more than anything, I vowel to not only be the best Mommy to your Sister but you as well. Mommy was not quite really ready for another kid, but I am ready and willing to do whatever it takes to make sure I keep the biggest smile on you and your sister's face and to make sure you both feel all the love that I have to give! It is such a surreal feeling to be a Mother of two but the strength that you and your Sister gives me (even though you have not gotten here just yet), I know I can tackle the world! I love you forever and always Mommy's stinky Mama two!

Love Always . . . Ma Ma

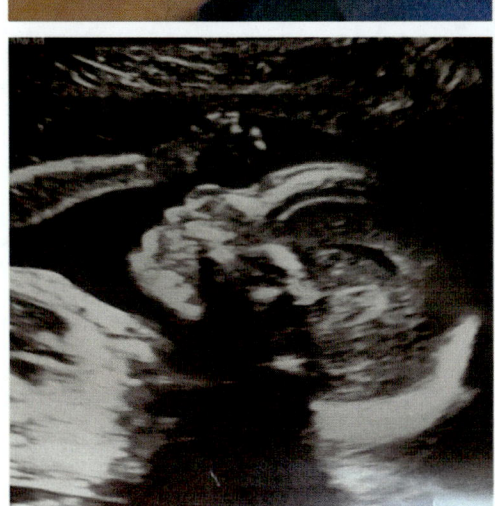

Note to My Black Daughter Erin, My Ladybug...

This is probably the most difficult note I will ever write to you baby Girl but not in a bad way, quite the contrary. You are my greatest creation, and my life would be incomplete without you. From the day we walked into the doctor's office to go through our first FET (frozen egg transfer), I knew I would be walking out carrying the most precious cargo I have ever carried. As you know Mommy had a hard time staying pregnant and I had to make some tough decisions, but I knew those sacrifices would lead to my special human. We made the decision to keep the sex of our embryo a secret until you were born, so I did not know you would be a Girl; I just knew I would love you with my whole heart. I knew I would make sure you walked through life knowing how much you were wanted and loved. I would make sure you understood you are enough, and your life matters because you are created in God's image and He does not make mistakes. You did not give me much trouble during my pregnancy either, but little did I know you would not enter this world easy. After 2.5 days of being in the hospital, being pumped with every induction medicine known, with no change in my cervix, I decided to have a C-section because you would not help Mommy out so we could meet you. However, even then you did not come out easy; you made the doctor come in and get you. I should have known then you were going to be stubborn like your Dad and dance to the beat of your own drum. Plus, I think you wanted to share my birthday month.

Fast forward 16 months and as I watch you grow and learn, I am in amazement. I step back most days and say "Yep, we did that!" Even when I am on my 5th hour of non-stop Sesame Street I cannot get enough of this feeling. I know they say you are your Dad's twin, but I see me in you in the most important ways. Even as a 1-year-old, you know what it means to be a good person. You are fearless, strong and very determined. As you know you are named after your great-grandfather and Abraham's wife. We knew when you picked your name, from the two options we gave, you would walk in the path of strength and faith and I pray daily that you keep that same energy.

So Many people wanted you to be here just as much as Mommy and Daddy, so always remember your village is strong and they are ready to love on you and pray for you when you need them. You will never have to second guess your purpose as we will, with the help of God, guide you down the path of greatness.

I could go on and on, but just remember the love in my heart is unconditional. I will always be there for you even when you think you will disappoint me. No conversation will be too hard for us to have. I am your sound board when you need to make the tough decisions. You will hate me some days but know I do everything out of love. You only get one Mom and you lucked out to get the best one.

Love Always...Mommy

A Note to My Black Daughter Hollie...

As a Woman who was raised with lots of love by her Grandmother, and surrounded by males; a loving husband, and a wonderful Son, I prayed for a Daughter to share the light and joy in my life, and God answered my prayers. Now that I am in my seventies, and you are in your forties, I can truly see your awesomeness. Not a person I know has a bigger, loving, caring heart for their family, friends, and community.

You continue to inspire me, and others, with your academic commitment in a world with glass ceilings for Black Women, and Men. In the 90's you left home, and headed nine hours away, to Hampton University in pursuit of an Engineering degree in a white male dominated field. Since then you have moved to a large city, married my son-in-law, tackled challenging jobs, and raised my three very smart grandchildren. You have continued to inspire their academic commitments resulting in one at the University of Chicago, and two others excelling in private schools. I see your inspiration and devotion to your children, and it is impeccable.

Your positive inspiration spreads infectiously through your community. I have seen the responses from your community members when you greeted children at the bus stop for thirteen years, served multiple times, at multiple schools as PTA president, chaperoned school field trips, taught religious education, led neighborhood events, and volunteered for other duties as needed in your community. Both the young and elderly have been recipients of your loving and encouraging personality.

Never, ever when you left home in 1991, did I think I would be this proud of you. And my friends thought that I was going to have a nervous breakdown, because we were so close. When you found residence in Maryland, and had my Grandchildren, together we stayed positive, and created a promise to each other that I would get to spend lots of time with my Grandchildren every year to ensure a generational bond with each of them. And this is a promise that you have faithfully kept. Together, as a Mother/Grandmother and Daughter we inspire and encourage our next generation. How awesome is that!

It did not matter which job you worked, on your way to work, you called me daily. Needless to say, that was the only time you had to talk, and you stayed positive and made it work. And now that I am in my seventies, you call more often so that if/when my mind becomes impaired, or if I become depressed, you will be able to detect it. During our talks, you always find the time to encourage your elderly mother to embrace and use technology. And daily you encourage me to keep moving by asking me "Mama, so what are you going to do today?".

Hollie stay positive and maintain your dignity, respect, esteem, worth, love and integrity, while being an inspiration to others. Continue to volunteer in the church, tithing and serving the Lord, and your blessings will keep coming.

Love Always...Mom

A Note to My Black Daughter, Valencia A. Mitchell (Angel)…

Angel, I remember the first day we met, you had on daisy dukes, tennis shoes and orange hair. It was two days before my birthday and I felt like God had answered my prayers and given me the Daughter that I always wanted. You entering my life made my complete set, I now had my Son and my Daughter.

You were a teenager and life had been unkind and I was blessed to invite you into my home. My goal was to raise both my children as my Mother raised my brother and I; with instilling the importance of love, faith, education, free will, decision making, self-respect and the value of your word. I was so excited to welcome you to the family that we quickly painted your bedroom your favorite color and I purchased us matching outfits to wear to church. I modeled "lady like" behavior. We got our hair and nails done on a regular basis. We worked out together, walked in the park and talked about Boys. We listened to music, cooked meals and had family movie nights. Early on, you asked me why I did all the things that I did for you. My answer simply was that you were a gift from God and that I did not take that responsibility lightly.

Over the years, I had the great joy of watching you transform from a tomboy to a beautiful Woman. I witnessed your baptism and acceptance of Christ as your personal savior. I consoled you when you were hurt, cheered for you when triumphed. I had a front-row seat as you discovered your own value system, priorities and boundaries. I had the privilege of being by your side as you ushered a beautiful baby boy into the world. I love seeing how you have developed into a wonderful, caring and protective Mother. Our relationship has not always been perfect, we had disagreements, took breaks and came back as if nothing ever happened as family often does.

Angel, I may not have given you birth to you; I love you just as if I had. I am thankful for the time (over 10 years) that we shared, and I look forward to Many more years (If God says the same).

I am grateful for the honor of calling you my Daughter.

I love you much!

Love Always…Ma

A Note to My Black Daughter Mia…

On a very cold 4th day of December in 2006, I waddled into a hospital in Illinois to welcome you to the world. You were very ready. Your personality was evident even in the womb. A very strong-willed, emotional, fighter came into the world. You made sure your voice was heard loud and clear. And the years that passed were no different. A personality that affectionately won you the nickname "Mama". Telling us how it should be before you could form words.

In a changing world, I pray that you can continue to be a voice that your generation needs. You have always been "beyond your years" in intelligence and maturity. Although, I wonder sometimes as we go through these teenage years. We have always known that you can do whatever you set your mind to. A born scholar, you have and continue to exceed all expectations which is why things you think are trivial are such a big deal to me. Choices you make early will set the tone for the rest of your life and we try to instill prosperous habits. Your drive and competitive nature are also amazing to me. You have the ability compete and excel at things you have never done before.

I am happy and sad that you are here at the time you are. I feel like this generation is right where you need to be. Adventurous, Intelligent, and Eclectic are the qualities that will take you far. I am happy because you were here to see someone who looks like you be president and vice president. So, when I tell you that you can do anything, there is evidence. When I push you harder you will know why. I am sad you had to see a civil rights movement come alive and the hate of this country on full display. I pray that it fuels your drive and makes you reach for so much more.

We are so proud to be your parents. You are developing into a beautiful, respectful, intelligent, strong-minded young lady and I cannot wait to see what you do! We love you "Mochalocious" and are so very proud of you.

Love Always…Mommy

A Note to My Black Daughters…

To my Princess Moriah, who is my second child…you are my little mini me. When I found out I was pregnant with you, I was so surprised! That same day I found out, I was already far along enough to know what the sex of the baby was too. It was one of the best days in my life; I was ready for you. You were born in Cleveland, Ohio at University Hospitals and now you are 6 years old. You are bright, responsible, and one of my biggest helpers. I am so thankful to God for blessing me with you. I encourage you, as a beautiful African American Princess to always do your best; I will always be rooting for you in anything you do. I am raising you to have confidence in yourself, and never let that confidence go. Always know that Mommy has your back; I will make every attempt to shield and guide you from any discriminations or weapons that come against you because I will always be there. I love your energy. I dedicate you to God and I dedicate my life to you and your siblings. If anyone tries to come against you and make you feel like you cannot do a job because of your race, tell them you are a child of a King. Moriah Deborah Limage, Mommy loves you so much. I cannot wait to see you grow and become a beautiful, Black, intelligent, successful Woman.

To my dearest baby Girl Isabel…oh how can I begin to explain just how precious you are to me. My tears will definitely flow. You were a special baby, born with a heart defect and a couple of other problems, but look at you now. You are such a strong baby, you fought through so much pain and several surgeries. It broke my heart, but thank God for keeping you strong. You are my baby always, my special baby. You already conquered so much and I know you will conquer much more in your life. I encourage you that Mommy will always be there for you. You are so smart, I love hearing you sing and talk and seeing you learn. As an African-American young Girl, your beauty is radiant. I will raise you to shine and live a positive life. Do not let anyone, especially for the cause of race, make you feel like you cannot do anything or that you are not good enough. Isabel Theanna Limage, Mommy loves you so much. I cannot wait to see you became a successful African-American Woman. I am so thankful for you baby Girl.

Love Always…Mommy

A Note to My Black Daughter, Jessica...

My wish is to provide you with all the positivity, encouragement, and inspiration that you will need to carry out the legacy that has been left for you, as well as add a little bit of your own. The Women before you have built a legacy that will stand the test of time. Sharing this legacy with you has been the best gift a Mother could ever receive. So great is the bond between a mother and her Daughter, and her Daughter, and her Daughter, and so on. Based on the legacy that you have been gifted, I pray that you will let the events in your life fuel your future with an abundant amount of greatness.

As you transition through this journey called life, continue to inspire others by being authentically you; gifted and talented, brilliant, beautiful, loving, powerful, creative, and strong. Maintain your dignity in all that you do. Spread positivity, respect, esteem, and love. When you start to feel like you do not fit in, or are different than the others, accept that you are different, you are unique, and you have a talent that God has given solely to you. Embrace your talents, and work on developing them into something God intended you to share with the world. The people around you may not understand your journey to embrace and develop your gift, and they do not need to because it is not for them. During stressful times, be mindful not to let your emotions overpower your intellect or become a distraction to the success and greatness I anticipate along your journey.

You were born with the ability to change people's lives, embrace your ability. Look around, look around, history is happening, and you just happen to be alive. Work to be young scrappy and hungry, and do not throw away your shot. Do not be afraid to holler just to be heard, because with every word you drop knowledge. And that my Daughter, is a fact. You have more knowledge than you can ever imagine. With every action you can make a difference. Let your beautiful heart guide you in your actions to share your gifts and talents with the world. When you hear that voice telling you that you will not make it, remember it is always darkest before the sunrise, and that is when it is time to super-bloom. No matter what, double or nothing, put your best face on, and go out with a bang.

Know that wherever God guides you on your journey, he will provide for you. Go the extra mile to leave a legacy because it is never crowded, but also know that you will never be alone. All the contributors in your legacy will always be with you. We have laid a strong foundation, we have given the world to you, and someday, you will blow us all away.

Remember "When you're gone who remembers your name? Who keeps your flame? Who tells your story?" – Alexander Hamilton

Love Always...Mom

Black Mom & Teen Daughter

Illustration By: Rodney Potts

A Note to Black Granddaughter, Janya, Juju, Jan, Ms. Mayer...

Although I have never birthed a child of my own, God gifted me with your Mother whom I love as if she were my own. When she had you, it was as if I finally had a baby. My first granddaughter, second grandchild. It appears as though we bonded instantly! Over the years, I have had the direct pleasure of watching you grow and develop into this independent, strong-minded, amazing young lady. Your advocacy for others is AMAZING! Your pride in your culture and heritage are far greater than mine when I was your age. Your relationship with your Mom is refreshing. The respect that you have for her sacrifices and perseverance to succeed is awesome. My prayer for you is to live life to its fullest. You are one of the most adventurous persons I know. Your willingness to travel and experience things if far reaching; continue to do just that! As you continue down this road called "life", know that there will be people you encounter that WILL NOT have your best interest at heart. Pray for direction when doubt creeps in because you are a CHILD of GOD, seek Him no matter what, especially when you are unsure. Why you seek HIM and He tells you "No", accept that and not "beat up" on yourself. Know that when God closes a door, it is in your best interest. Know that you will encounter struggles along the path of life, embarrass them and know that they are tests that lead to your testimonies. To me, your name represents:

<u>J</u>aunty

<u>A</u>mazing

<u>N</u>atural

<u>Y</u>oung

<u>A</u>wesome

Always remember that your Granny will always love you to the moon and back!

Love Always... Granny

A Note to My Black Daughters, Dawn (Dee Dee) and Zora (Zee)...

Dawn: *I am confident that your style and grace will one day help to catapult you into a dancer or a career goal that makes you shine. I love that you spread joy to your family and friends. You wake up every day, ready to face the world with a positive attitude. I also love that you like to have fun and that you live for juicy "tea" or gossip. Your curiosity is demonstrated in your thirst for learning when you are doing your schoolwork, as well as with the people you encounter in the world around you. I hope you will continue to nurture that trait.*

Zora: *You are smart and fearless. You run towards things that make you nervous and you persevere. Your energy will make you a great dancer, musician or chef. You are such a great friend to those around you and our own family comedian. You love to make people laugh, but you are honest about the world around you. I hope you will continue to speak your truth.*

I am so proud of both of you. I love you very much. I want you to know that I will also be here to encourage you. You are the dream that your Grandmothers and Great-Grandmothers hoped for future generations. I want you to know that you will face challenges but will get through it. Sometimes challenges can bring you closer to what you really want. I also hope that you know that it is important to have fun and to love yourself. That will help you get through those times when you may question what you are experiencing in life. I hope that you will have a loving, supportive partner like I do with your Dad.

I am happy to be your Mom and cherish all the adventures that we have had together. We have had fun at museums, movie nights, concerts in the park and Many home dance parties.

You have been there to cheer me on for business plan competitions and teaching journalism. You have helped me want more for myself as a Woman and encouraged me to fully be myself-- flaws and all. Both of you are the reasons that I create magazines for Girls and why I continue to work for organizations that help Girls and youth live their lives with confidence. Thank you for helping me gain my purpose. You have more than Black Girl Magic, you have Black Girl Power and Confidence.

Love Always...Mom

A Note to My Black Daughter, Robyn, My Poohbutt…

You have always been my reason to never give up. You are the meaning of a true first love. You are everything a Mother could dream and hope for. You have seen Mama struggle but you have NEVER seen me give up. These are all the things, as you grow into a Woman, I want to instill in you. You have already come so far and learned so much; it is only one place for you to go and that is among the stars where you belong. God broke the mold when He made you. Get better as each day goes by, get wiser, but most important, stay my Beautiful, Black Daughter.

Love Always…Mama

A Note to My Black Daughters Melissa Paige and Robyn Danielle...

Never, ever forget that I love you with my whole heart. I love you in good times and in the not so good times. My prayer is that you would let God lead you in all of your decisions always keeping him first. I pray that you would be the best you, you can possibly be. In everything you do, do it in excellence. Melissa and Robyn, you are beautiful, strong, brave, bold, courageous and resilient Women. Do not let anything or anyone stop you from reaching your dreams and goals. You each have a character all your own. Be individually who God wants you to be and as you all come into the Women God wants you to be, may you find your every heart's desire. You will face challenges in life, just know that life isn't about waiting for the storm to pass....it is really and truly about learning to dance in the rain. Every day may not be good, but if you find something good in every day, I promise your day will be better. Live your lives freely and to the fullest. Do not be afraid to take chances. If you fail the first time, try again and again and again! Fail forward, but just simply failing, is not an option. Be proud of your African American heritage for you are two beautiful Black Queens and should be treated as such. If anybody does not recognize that, then they should not be in your lives. Be very careful who you surround yourselves with and know that you are braver than you believe, stronger than you seem, and smarter than you think! No matter what and if we are ever apart, know that your Mama will always be with you!!!

Melissa and Robyn, you are life's greatest gift to me and I will forever treasure this gift God has given to me. Remember to laugh, to love and most of all....to live your lives to the fullest believing that all things are possible through Christ. I love and adore you forever and always!!

Love Always...Mommy

A Note to My Black Bonus Daughters Krystle, Candace and Ciara...

I did not give you life but life gave me you and it is a privilege to call you my Daughters. While I know I am not your biological Mom, (I would never take that away from her), I am thankful that I get to be a part of your lives and watch you grow into young Women Candace and Ciara. Krystle, I am thankful that I get to watch you grow as a Mother yourself who is now raising her own children. Thank you that I get to be Grandma to those beautiful babies of yours. I may not have been there the day you were born but you became mine when a new family formed. Some blessings come sooner and others come later, having you in our family is only an additional blessing from God. You all are smart, funny, intelligent and beautiful. Candace and Ciara, I am so impressed with the young Ladies you are becoming. Krystle, I am so impressed with the strong educated Woman you have become. Always strive for excellence in everything you do and be the best you, you can possibly be. Know that you are loved, accepted, appreciated and adored. Know that you belong and you will always fit in, for you were sent from God above and he does not make mistakes. It is not flesh and blood but love that makes us family. Thank you for allowing me to love you as my own and I pray God's covering over your lives all the rest of your days! I love you forever and always!!!

Love Always...Mommie K/Kim

A Note to My Black Daughter (Clo Bug) Chloe...

I am so blessed to be your Mom and grateful I get to share one of my (Many) notes to you with the world. Everything about you happened in an orderly, peaceful, and scientific way. Your Brother really wanted a sibling, your Dad and I agreed it made sense for our family to grow. I will never forget when I went in for my annual checkup that February, I thought I had lost a lot of weight. My doctor predicted that you would be born on Thursday, November 25, 2010. When I checked my calendar-that date was going to be Thanksgiving Day that year. I worked on the best team at my job when I was pregnant with you and was able to work until the day before you were born with minimal stress. It was neat that you were born as predicted. You have made it a point to always be on time from your entry into the world. I loved bringing you home on Black Friday that year. I will always enjoy the holiday season so much more since your birth, knowing your birthday is one month away from Christmas Day!

When you were in the third grade your teacher shared that you were having trouble writing but you were doing very well in all your other subjects. You shared with me that it was your goal to get straight "A's" in school and one day become a doctor like your Aunt. I see your passion for science, math, and technology to engineer things that function in your room and in the real world. I am energized to see your excitement about beauty, skin care and chemistry; I'm so proud to see your desire to examine different specimen under your microscope. It was cool to watch you walk around Beautycon LA the last few years; you did your best to make beauty and skin care make sense. I believe make up use is personal preference and there is a ton of science and statistics to test theories of what it means to "prefer" one look over another. Keep exploring the world to find your niche, I will love you no matter what you decide to do.

As you become a young Woman, I can see how your growth is exponential in comparison to your classmates. I pushed for you to go to Kindergarten as soon as you turned five years old. Your height now allows you to tower over most of your classmates and you are the youngest person in your class (smile). As I look at your mid-year report card for the fifth grade and see that you achieved your goal of getting all "A's" (during a pandemic), I am so proud of you. It took hard work, determination, and dedication to achieve your goal. To be honest — you and your Brothers have done something that your Dad and I just did not do. All three of you have gotten top marks (all "E" s or "A" s) in school!

Thanks for getting me back to teaching the youth at church. We both love the story of Moses and how he became a great leader of the Israelites. In closing I would like to encourage you with Moses' words found in Deuteronomy 31:6 (KJV), "Be strong and of good courage..." You are a star in my eyes; so, please do not let anyone dim your light or steal your shine.

Love Always...Mom

A Note to My Black Daughter, Princess Joi…

You are my firstborn, my beautiful, most precious gift. I am truly amazed at your talents and gifts already visible at the tender age of two and a half! You are going to be something great — an actress, a dancer, a writer, a doctor —whatever your heart desires. I believe that one of your gifts in life is to make others smile just as you do for me each and every day. You are sweet, kind, unique, smart, funny, and loving. I know that you will make a large imprint in this world. My prayer for you is that you will always love God with all of your heart, lean on Him for understanding, and allow Him to direct your path. I will always love you, support you, cheer for you, and do my best to protect you.

Dream BIG and reach for the stars. You can be or do anything you put your mind to, as long as you keep God first and stay humble. I am so excited to see how God is going to bless your life and how Many lives you will bless just by being in their midst. You are my sweet angel and I am so honored that God has chosen me to be your Mom!

I need you to know that it will not always be easy. Unfortunately, there are people in this world who do not want you, a Black Girl/Woman, to succeed and will try to sabotage your success. They may talk about you, demote you, or belittle your abilities. But know that you are fearfully and wonderfully made, and what God has for you, no one can hinder you. Always remember that you are special, beautiful, and loved and you can do all things through Christ who strengthens you!

Love Always…Mommy

A Note to My Black Daughter, Brianna, "Bri Bri", My Heart Beat…

Words cannot express how much I love you. When I was 35 years old God blessed me with you and boy where you a miracle baby. First, I had a hard time getting pregnant until fertility helped, then I was in a bad car accident in my 4th month of pregnancy with an 18 wheeler truck and you were just fine, then at 1-year-old when you were just learning how to walk, your left leg would not bend and found out you had hip dysplasia and had to where a cast for 6 months… BUT GOD you where healed, and to look at you today and the young Lady you are growing you to be today is amazing.

It is amazing to see how talented and smart you are. When you discovered how much you loved the arts you just took off with it. From dancing to the love of digital design. You think outside the box and see things so different that it just absolutely blows my mind to where I admire that gift about you. I pray that all your dreams come true and God blesses you with all your hearts desires in life.

I always want you to remember to always lean on God in all that you do. Remember to always love yourself and love the beautiful Black skin you are in. Your character is what defines you and as you grow in life and learn things along always about yourself. Never, loose yourself and the beautiful Black young Lady that God has created you to be. I am so proud of you and thank God that He chose me to be your Mom.

Love Always…Mommy

A Note to My Black Daughter, Jacora A.K.A. Gusana…

When I met your Dad, he shared a recurring dream he had for years. In short, it was of a little Girl who was adventurous, outspoken, and beyond witty. He referred to her as Little Miss. Fourteen years later, Little Miss has successfully tricked her beloved G-Pa into skipping Pre-school, hiked through muddy creeks- fully dressed, set traps to save the neighborhood from backyard clowns, and written tear-jerking plays. Your Dad and I prayed that you would be energetic, strong, and kind. You are living way beyond our expectations.

Right before my eyes I am witnessing a developing Christian, a watchful Sister, a caring Granddaughter, Niece, and Cousin, a helpful neighbor, and a role model student.

I love that you define you! I love that you acknowledge right from wrong. I love that you stick up for the little Man. I love that you entertain yourself to the beat of your own djembe. I love that you read a diverse genre of literature and your circle of friends reflect so. I love your confidence to make mistakes and grow from them.

You are beautiful when you simultaneously rock your plaid and polka-dots. You are beautiful when you are deliriously sleepy and start rambling about the world until you drift off. You are beautiful when you sing like no one can hear you, but your voice echoes through the vents. No comment about your joke telling…

You stand on the shoulders of Women who sacrificed for you to live. Happy. Educated. Hopeful. Their efforts were not in vain. These Women are your Great-Grandmothers and Grandmothers, your namesakes. You are a legacy vessel of their ambition and vision.

Continue advocating for yourself, forward thinking, developing, and fine tuning your craft within your wood designing business and playwriting. Create. Create. Create. Write. Write. Write. You have tapped into a skillset that will inspire others towards their goals, promote unity amongst a people, and the impact of presence.

I thank you for this remarkable experience of being your Mom. If no one ever tells you, please know, you are amazing, capable, and more than enough!

Your life matters. Your mind matters. Your dreams matter.

Your future is scintillating with promise and the world better invest in a pair glasses that are three layers thick.

"When you mess with the Goose, you get pecked!"

Love you today, tomorrow, and forever!

Love Always…Mom

A Note to My Black Daughter, Saige…

From the day that I found out I was pregnant; the emotions of fear and joy filled my heart. Knowing that I was going to be a Mom to a Daughter was one of my biggest dreams come true. The first time I held you in my arms I knew God had blessed me with a special gift. I knew God had heard every prayer for you before you came to be. God knew exactly what I needed in a Daughter, and gave me that in you. You are such a loving baby. Your actions speak much louder than the words you yet know how to express. My prayer is that you continue to love people…but most importantly, that you love God first. As you navigate through life there are a few things that I want you to remember.

God is the only constant in your life, so value your relationship with him above all else. Saige you will have seasons in your life where things are going to go great and others where it will feel as though the world is caving in around you. God says that He will never leave you nor forsake you (Deuteronomy 31:6) and that His promises will always hold true (Isaiah 55: 10-11). Therefore, follow God without hesitation. When you do not know what to do… seek God. Read His word, pray, and obey with the faith that God is going to do what He said He will do.

Do not let the world define who you are, find your identity in Christ. You are fearfully and wonderfully made by the One who created the universe. Although you are beautiful on the outside, know true beauty will always radiate from the inside. It will come from the love of Christ you exhibit towards others, how you handle difficult situations, your integrity and always choosing to walk in humility. There is freedom in not living up to the world's standard, walk in it. Make sure you understand the value and importance of guarding your heart. The Bible says to guard your heart above all else for out of it flows the issues of life (Proverbs 4:23). The condition of your heart will impact your emotions, and they guide your thoughts, words, and actions. Make sure you use all three to bless and not to tear down. This world may try to break you, but that does not give you the right to break it back.

Lastly, live your life in a way in which you will leave this world better than you found it. Know the expectation is not perfection, but that you pursue the best you. When you make mistakes learn from them. In all that you do remember you represent Christ and your number one goal is to draw others to Him. I am not sure what this Mother-Daughter journey will bring, but I am looking forward to guiding you along the way and teaching you how to navigate Womanhood. Just know that I love you more than words can ever express, but that God loves you more!

Love Always…Mommy

A Note to My Black Daughters Sheryl & Kim…

On March 19, 1963, my husband and I welcomed our first-born Daughter. He insisted on naming her, so I relented. He named her Sheryl Lynn Thomas. We were so happy to have this little bundle of joy in our lives. She was all we could have hoped for. Then, three months later to our surprise, we found out we were going to be parents again. So, on June 19, 1964, we welcomed our second Daughter Kimberly Yvonne Thomas. Needless to say, Sheryl was not very happy. Kim's first day home, Sheryl hit her in the head with her bottle. But as time passed, Sheryl became a great Sister. She took this job very seriously. She became Kim's protector in every way. Kim relished being the baby and was so happy to have a big Sister to look after her.

Their Dad and I were very blessed to have these beautiful Girls. Even though they are only 15 months apart, they are quite different. Sheryl is a leader in every way, who is not shy about speaking her mind. Kim, being the baby, is a little more laid back. She depends on Sheryl a lot. But, if you ruffle her feathers, she will set you straight 'quick and in a hurry'.

We raised our Daughters to be strong Black Women. We assured them that they could accomplish anything they aspired to. We taught them to never lose hope despite the cruelties of this world. We let them know that it would take daily positive thinking to remind themselves that they are unique, gifted, and worthy.

We raised them to be God fearing Women and to always put God first. We warned them that life is not always fair, but if they keep their faith, they will survive whatever befall them. I am so proud of my Daughters, my beautiful Black Queens. They are incredibly brilliant in every way. I thank God for them each day. Stand tall my beautiful Queens. Always know that I am your biggest fan and will forever be there to support you in every way.

Love Always…Mom

A Note to My Black Daughter Dionna Patrice Cooper...

To my first born, Dion. You are an amazing Daughter and Mother, and I could not image my life without you. You have a sweet spirit; loving heart, and are passionate about helping others. As a single Mom raising a Daughter, only God know how frightened I was to as a single Mom. Afraid that I would not get this Motherhood thing right. Afraid that something would happen to you while you were out of my sight. Uncertain that I could provide for you financially. All these things raced through my head daily. The hope that I had in raising you alone was the fact that your Grandmother's voice, assuring me that I was not raising you alone. She was there in the beginning until her departure from this Earth. You were her Chocolate Drop. The assurance of her calm voice helped me to persevere. With that same voice I speak to you today. Reminding you that you are someone special. Despite life's challenges, obstacles that have gotten in your way and failed relationships, you need to know that it is not over and there is a happy ever after for you. Let the Lord guide your path and take Him at His word. He will not leave you, nor forsake you. He is a present help in time of need. And your steps are ordered by Him. I am often reminded of a special time in your life when you asked me to perform with you at a talent show. You were afraid to do it alone and other classmates had already picked their partners. I was honored that you requested my support. We sang the song HERO by Mariah Carey and it was beautiful. I am reminded of that day even now and it brings tears to my eyes. Because life has challenged you to, I have listened to that song and I have come to understand that the song was words of prophecy that ring in my ear to this day. A constant reminder that a hero lies in YOU. Now go and be the giant that you are! Jeremiah 29:11 I am extremely proud of you and the Mother you have become. Love you forever - Love you for always.

Love Always...Mommy

A Note to My Black Daughter Kara Latrice Smith...

To my second oldest Daughter, Kara-Kara. You are a ray of sunshine, always smiling even when you feel like crying. You have an inner peace about you that cannot be described. People are drawn to you for that very reason. You are a perfect balance of me, and your dad and it works for you. Your laughter and bright smiles tend to brighten up a room as you enter in. God's light illuminates your space, use this anointing to glorify Him. The Bible tells us to let our light shine before Men that they see our good works and exalt our Father in heaven. Keep your light shining and do not let anyone dull your shine. Your life has not been without challenges; however, your tenacity has pulled you through. As a Mom, your fight has gotten stronger, and stronger, although Many times you felt defeated. I am here to tell you that the race is not given to the strong, but rather to those that endure to the end. Keep pushing my Child, life will get easier and times will get better. Let the voice from within speak louder, and louder until the enemy's voice can no longer be heard. You are a mighty force to be reckoned with and one day soon, all your hard work will pay off. You are amazing and I love you so much. Stay focused and be the best that you can be. I am always rooting for you. There is a winner in you!! Philippians 4:13 I am extremely proud of the Woman and Mother you have become. Love you forever - Love you for always!

Love Always...Mommy

A Note to My Black Daughter Kiyona LaChe' Smith...

To my youngest Daughter, Kiyona (Tooter) you are so special, so brilliant, gifted, and talented. The sky is the limit to what you can achieve. It is time for you to soar! Do not be afraid to fly, you can do it, I know you can. And if you fall, get back up quickly, and try it again. Falling does not make you a failure; you only fail if you never try. Pray about everything and let the spirit of the Lord lead you through. My prayer for you is that one day soon, the pain and disappointment of your past will disappear and the thought of it will not hurt you anymore. People can be cruel, and revenge is easy to do. I love that fact that you always take the high road and let the naysayers be to themselves. This is your season for grace and favor. You will reap what you have sown, and greatness will meet you on your road to success.

I encourage you to seek Him first, and your plans, dreams and goals will be successful. Let the Lord lead you and you will be just fine. You are a mighty force to be reckoned with and your latter days will be brighter than the former days. You will look up and the pain from your past will not hurt you anymore. Their unwillingness to accept you as a friend is their loss, not yours! Matthew 16:22 I got you and most importantly God has you! Love you forever - Love you for always.

Love Always...Mommy

Black Mom & Adult Daughter

Illustration By: Rodney Potts

A Note to My Black Daughters Alyssa and Keiara, My Girls…

You two are the best things that ever happened to me, my greatest accomplishments. You mean the world to me and as you know I would give the world for you. Now that you are both grown, we can look back and laugh at so Many fun, happy and even sad memories as we continue to make new ones. Throughout your childhoods, I tried my best to make it the best times of your lives. I never wanted you to worry about anything. I wanted you to enjoy your childhood and experience new adventures. Together, we learned that our happy place is the beach; those were some of our favorite vacations. As you both continue to mature and become your own Woman, it is my wish that you will continue to be the best YOU that you can be. You two can do anything you put your hearts and mind to. Remember, I have always told you both that you can do and be anything you want to. I am so looking forward to the days when there are little Keiara's and Alyssa's giving you all of what you given me and then some. You Girls are going to be wonderful wives and mothers. I pray that I have given you a good blueprint to follow.

Remember to trust God and let Him lead you. I know you will do great things.

Love Always…Mommy

A Note to My Black Daughter Aaliyah, My Ladybug...

The first day I laid eyes on you, I knew no love like this! You were so tiny and I cried because of what I knew lie ahead of you. Together we endured and today I am amazed at the young Woman you are. We have had conversations about life and things that are inexplicable; 2020 was a tough year for you emotionally with all of the injustices, and like the empath you are, you immediately made the connection to your Dad. It was hard but my constant reassurance made things much easier to handle. I want you to know that you can come to me with ANYTHING that is bothering you or makes you feel uncomfortable because I will ease you pain and protect you with every part of me.

I want you to know that there will be times that people will not like you just because of how you look. It could be the color of your skin or your beautiful hair. If you ever have to experience this, it is important to NEVER blame yourself or dislike the way you look. You are beautiful inside and out. The last thing you should do is let someone else's biased opinion of how you look dictate how you carry yourself and force you to change your looks. You are BEAUTIFUL! You are AMAZING! Most importantly, you are LOVED!

Love Always...Mama

A Note to My Black Daughter, Kqiera DeVine, My DeVine, My Baby Girl...

It took 3 times to get you and I finally did! You were my own personal baby doll. I got to dress you up, play in your hair and take you with me everywhere! It has been an honor and a pleasure to watch you grow into a beautiful, caring, personable, outgoing Daughter and a warm, loving, caring Mother. I am so proud of you DeVine! I only wish you could see you the way I do. You have so much talent and so much potential that you have yet to tap into. Once you do, the world will be yours! You have the power to command what you want and receive it! Step into that power baby!!! You are such a blessing to so Many and you do not even know it! Imagine what you could do once you step into your power! So, hold your head up, reach for the stars, set your intentions and Manifest that shit, because you can!!! I love you to life My DeVine and it is truly a blessing to be your Mom!

Love Always...Mommy

A Note to My Black Daughter, My SaSa, My Niece/Daughter Sacia...

You were my 1st baby! And you survived (lol). Your Mom used to let me comb your hair and I swear I would put every BoBo in your hair that I could find! (LMAO) And then everywhere I went (except the club) you would be with me!! Everyone knew you!! Some knew you as my Niece, some knew you as my Daughter! And I will not even mention when I had you on the back of a motorcycle with me at the age of 3!! (I told your Mom that after you were grown) But you liked it!! (haha) Sacia, I love you so very much! You did actually prep me for my baby Girl and I am grateful for that, but not only that, we have such a close bond now and I cherish every Moment that we spend together. I have watched you grow into a confident, courageous, beautiful Woman and I am excited to see what is coming in this next chapter of your life!! I love you My SaSa!

Love Always...Auntie

Made with Frames

A Note to My Black Grand Daughter, Pumpkin, Aniyah Sadaqa…

My name sake, My Pumpkin, my seer. I have known love but the love that a Big Mama has for her Grandbabies is indescribable and you were the first one to show me that! From the Moment my eyes met yours, I was head over heels in love with you! There is nothing that I would not do to see you smile Pumpkin. I am so excited to see where life takes you on your journey and how God uses your gift of sight. Always remember that Big Mama loves you and will always be with you in spirit! I love you to life My Pumpkin.

Love Always…Big Mama

A Note to My Black Grand Daughter, Shuga, McKenize Simone…

My Shuga, Shuga! You are my mystical baby. When I first looked in your eyes, I saw so much love but I also saw a mystic in you. That was confirmed when you told me you knew who Nana was and you had never met her in the physical but I knew she had come to you in the spirit realm. You are my sensitive baby. I cannot wait for you to begin using your gifts! I will be waiting to help you and Pumpkin on your journeys. I love you so very much My Shuga!

Love Always…Big Mama

A Note to My Black Grand Daughter, Pebbles, My Rayn…

My Pebbles, when I looked in your eyes I saw so much joy, but also a seriousness in you. You are my gifted baby! You are an angel of few words but with a powerful glare and a pure heart! You have dealt with meds and surgery and you have overcome both. You are so powerful and so strong and I admire that in you. Your life will be so amazing and interesting!! I am really excited to watch your journey and see you transform into the Amazing Woman that you will be!! Big Mama will always be with you and by your side!! I Love you my Rayn Drop.

Love Always…Big Mama

A Note to My Black Daughter Noelle, My Britt…

The day you entered the world my life changed. November 7th 1991 at 1:42pm, I learned that life and my purpose was bigger than me. You were an easy baby, happy with a big smile. Who knew this 21-year-old new Mom could raise a queen. I had no idea how life would treat you. I just knew that life was unfair and I wanted to protect you.

I did my best Noelle. I tried to give you what I had and what I did not have. I wanted you to have the confidence and self-esteem I did not have at an early age. You were strong, self-assured, and decisive; all the things I was not as a young Girl. You were a rock star in high school. A head cheerleader, a class leader, musician, singer, and of course your favorite title Eric's big Sister. You made it through those hard high school years, and no one even knew we were broke when you won homecoming queen. Thank God for Grandma, without her during those lean times I do not know how we would have made it. I could not have raised you without her. Her example, influence, prayers, and 'speaking the truth in love' has helped cultivate you into the Woman you are today. There is no way I can take credit alone for you. It took a village of family, friends, the church, and the Beachwood community.

You were the queen for the 2010 class. An honor well deserved. You winning homecoming queen was Gods way of reminding me He still had us and He had not forgotten us. Ever since you were born, God has been coming through for us. He provided every step of the way. I remember trying to figure out how I was going to get you through UC those four years and He made a way. Then God supplied the scholarship for your graduate degree at OSU. All I can say is But God; He is truly El Shaddai. Never doubt Him! He will always provide for you.

Poodie (that silly name), I want the best for you. As a Woman and especially as a Black Woman life can be rough for us. I want you to hold on to your dreams. Take risks and do not play it safe. Abandon yourself to God and your plans will succeed.

I know you are almost 30 years old and you are wondering God, where is my Boaz? You want to be a Mother and have a family. Just know He sees you. He is maturing your husband and at the same time He is maturing you. Trust His process, obey His word, seek first His kingdom and nothing will be withheld from you. It is all on the way, wait on Him, rest in Him, and stay in your lane.

I love you Britt, and I am a better Mother and Woman because of you. Thanks for being Eric's real Mom (lol) and thanks for being patient with me and loving me always. One day, I will be able to pay for being my IT support, editor, and executive assistant. Always know, Girl I got you! You are my pride & joy! Matthew 6:33, Proverbs 16:3, & Psalm 37:4

Love Always…Mom

A Note to My Black Daughter My Dearest Megan…

Did I ever tell you that your Dad and I spent our entire pregnancy believing you, our first child, was going to 100% be a boy? I mean we knew nothing of gender neutrality at that time as we do now. So, everything we had was designed for a boy including the clothing we received at your baby shower. It tickles me because after 17 hours of labor, a little girl showed up. We were all shocked. That still makes me laugh. And in that moment, we called your name for the first time…and it would be Megan Lynn Smith.

As you already know, your middle name Lynn is the same as my middle name. But what you most likely do not know is that 'Megan' is of Welsh origin and means 'Pearl' which also translates to 'Child of Light'. How so very perfect is the name Megan for YOU. In the Bible, Matthew 13:45 states "Again, the kingdom of heaven is like a merchant seeking fine pearls." Matthew uses pearls as a symbol for the kingdom of heaven which is perfect because a fine pearl is a precious treasure that needs no refining or cutting by man. It comes to us perfect and lustrous created by God via nature, as is the kingdom of heaven, which only God can create and perfect. You, my dear Megan, were created perfectly as a Child of Light. You are wise beyond your years, and always have been. You are a light that draws others toward you and that guides those that may be lost. You are a light for those that are hurting and for those that are filled with joy. Megan, a 'Child of Light' — how perfect is that description.

As you continue growing and shining, you will see that some in this world may not see your light. It will be due to their own blinders such as bigotry and other phobias, none of which have anything to do with you and who you are. Do not let their ignorance stop you from shinning your light. Also, you will see that some will ask you to dim your light complaining that it is too bright. Do not let their self-esteem issues affect your desire to continue shining. Never make yourself small so that others can feel big.

'Megan', 'Pearl', 'Child of Light'. You. Continue my dear heart being true to you, passionate about following your dreams, and dedicated to making this sometimes-cruel world a better place for all. Continue always being that bright light. I love you my oldest baby to the moon and back times infinity.

Love Always…Mom

A Note to My Black Daughter Carnesha…

My dearest baby girl, I thank God for blessing me with such a beautiful, smart, outgoing, considerate, loving, caring, creative, fashionista diva of a Daughter. You are definitely everything I asked God for in a Daughter. I love you and it is my prayer that God continues to bless you and keep you!!!

Love Always…Mommy

A Note to My Black Daughter, Aubree...

Aubree Sky, my gift from God. You have been a ball of excitement, energy, and joy from day one. You never cease to amaze me! I am elated by your intelligence and eagerness to learn. I love that you are fearless and courageous of everything but a fly hahaha.

This might sound mean, but I do not want you to have what I did not have growing up. The "things" I did not have growing up made me work harder and trust God. I was surrounded by people who loved and cared for me and taught me that, whatever I do for Christ would last and everything else is a waste.

So, Aubree, it is my duty and honor to take care of you, love you, and surround you with people that will help guide you on the right path. When your Dad and I had your dedication ceremony at church, we surrendered you to Christ and this gives me peace that you will be a successful Woman of God.

Love Always...Mommy

A Note to My Black Daughter, To My Sweet Stepbaby Te'Ari...

I am so thankful that I have been entrusted with being your "other" mother. I admire how you are so independent but remain willing to listen and learn. I love how you have always felt comfortable with talking to me. I adore the countless laughs we share. I love you for always welcoming my presence, opinion, and advice. I love your inner and outer beauty. I love your humbleness, your work ethic, your toughness and your sensitivity. I am proud of you and I love you.

Love Always...Stephanie

A Note to My Black Daughter, To My Firstborn Baby Micah...

I thank God for appointing me to lead and follow you on this journey called life. I love how sweet and spicy you are. I love your sensitivity, your compassion for others and your willingness to always take a stand against injustices. I love you for always making me laugh and accepting the fact that I'm probably going to cry. I love your internal and external beauty. I adore how you are comfortable in the skin you're in and never feel pressured to conform to anything else. You make me proud in all that you do.

Love You...from Moy

A Note to My Black Daughter, To My Littlest Baby Girl Robbie...

You are so beautiful, so smart, and so talented that it amazes me. I love that you are not afraid to try anything. I love your rambunctiousness, humbleness, kindness, athleticism, and your natural ability to lead. I love you for teaching me that each daughter needs a different version of her mother and I adore that ONLY YOU can make me be comfortable with being all touchy-feely. I pray that you continue being the sweet person you are today, so that you can continue to add kindness to the world.

Love Forever, Mommy

A Note to Each of My Black Daughters...

Always treat yourself with love and kindness. Protect your mind, body, and spirit. Pray. Be proud of yourself. Admit your mistakes. Forgive yourself. Save some money. Have good credit. Learn to love and when to let go. Always remember that actions speak louder than words. I love each of you so much and I cannot wait to see what marks you leave on the world.

A Note to My Black Daughter, My Dear Kennedi...

As I write this note to you, I am just full. I cannot believe you are 18 and in a few short months, will embark on your own journey. What gives me peace and fills me with joy is knowing the young Woman that you have become. You are as independent thinking as they come! You are beautiful, funny, quirky, loving and so Many other things. You simply light up the room with your smile. As we have watched you grow, I have done my very best in being intentional to teach you everything to mold you onto a Christ loving Woman of integrity and grace.

While I watched you grow, I grew too. I still want to protect you, while I know I cannot shield you from everything, you are always covered. From a very young age I taught you to love your hair, your skin and value who you are every day. Always view yourself, not by this world's standards, but as a Woman who is fearfully and wonderfully made in God's image. I wanted you to learn from my mistakes and understand that triumphs often come with a fight. Never give up! I love that you have learned to advocate for yourself. I love that you know your worth! As you guard your heart, I pray you encounter Many good people on your journey who deserve your trust. Remember it is okay to keep your circle small. Enjoy life sweet Girl!

I want you to know that you never have to compromise who you are to be successful. Allow God to lead you in all the decisions you make. Remember when things get difficult that your ability to overcome is not just about you-it is about Him and how you live for His glory. Raising Girls is not easy, raising a young Lady is even more difficult, especially today. I know you are going to do tremendous things in your life that make this world better for yourself and those around you. Do not be afraid to make mistakes, they are practice for success. Never be afraid to ask questions and be curious. Always know that we are here for you and with you no matter where you go. We are excited about God's plans for your life. Jeremiah 29:11. God's favor and protection always!

So proud of you!

Love Always...Mom (and Dad) ❤

A Note to My Black Daughter, Aubrey Marie...

I thank God each day that he saw fit to make me your Mother. I was filled with pure joy from the very Moment that I knew you were coming into my life. I fell in love you with you instantly when I stared into your eyes for the very first time. God blessed me with such a perfect angel. I clapped the loudest when you took your first steps and sobbed like a baby on your first day of your kindergarten. Today, I continue to be in awe of the young person you are growing into being. Your passion for adventure, spark for creativity, compassion for others, and innate curiosity to learn all things brings warmth and laughter to everyone around you.

I truly mean it when I say you have made my life so much better. I cannot wait to get home to see your face and hear about your day. You have given my life so much purpose as I strive to be your role model by working hard to excel professionally and being a steward of our community.

I urge you to always keep God at the center of your life; with God, all things are possible. Remember that things may not be always be easy, and others may not treat you fairly or with the respect and dignity you deserve as a young Black Woman, but it is at these times, you must stand your tallest and draw upon the strength of your character and rich legacy of all the strong African American Women before you. There may be times when others may say you are not good enough or you are not pretty enough. Do not let them distract you from what is true and right. You are absolutely beautiful and intelligent, and yes, your life matters.

Aubrey, you make me so happy and so proud to be your Mother. I love you like I have loved no other being. I promise to always protect you, support you, inspire you, challenge you, but most importantly offer you my all enduring unconditional love. God bless you my beautiful baby Girl.

Love Always... Mommy

A Note to My Black Daughter, Madison Tayha-Linet Reid, My Baby Bird...

You have always been the joy of my life. From the Moment you entered this world, with a boisterous cry, to this current "Girl is on fire movement," you have and will continue to set this world a blaze.

I know every Mom thinks they have a "one-of-a-kind child," but, Madison, you are that 1 in a Million. You are the daughter of dreams. When I look at you I can only thank God for this blessing. You are the best part of me, the yin to my yang! You have my "DNA", but what makes me so proud is how your personality reflects the spirit of our ancestors. Your confidence and strength resonates through your humility and courage you share with the world. Daily you walk in the wisdom of your grandparents, the beauty of your aunts, the generosity of uncles, and laughter of your relatives.

You are a triple threat "Beauty, Brains, and Talent". From your first place modeling awards, to your world recognition of the "world needs books," to the current theatrical appearances and motivational speeches, you are the epitome of success!

Be the best "unapologetically you"! You are fiercely made by God with strength, courage, resilience, and tenacity. Know whatever you want in life "go for it". Yes, you will stumble and may even fall, but do not let that defeat you...the African Proverb states "Not everyone who chased the zebra caught it, but he/she who caught it, chased it".

I tell you often-do not change who you are so others can like you...stay you, so the right people can love you! Love you deeply, passionately, and unconditionally. Know your friends like you know yourself. Your generosity will attract Many but do not allow your heart to be the pied piper to the insecure, vexed, and narcissistic of the world. And always extend the hand back to bring another sister up.

You know why I initially called you "Bird" but now, I have another reason. It is for you to spread your mighty wings and soar. I see your brilliance, your enthusiasm, and how you deeply care for others. I am so very proud of you now, and the Woman you are becoming. The world is what YOU make it. So, make this world better than you came into it.

One day I will not be on this earth, but I want you to know it has been my HONOR and PRIVILEGE to be your mother. I love you always and FOREVER!

Love Always...Mommy, Tracy Reid

A Final Note to All the Black Daughters…

There are a few things we want you to always remember as you, our Black Daughters, continue on this journey called life:

- *Always pray and keep God first in EVERYTHING you do.*
- *You are always enough!*
- *I will ALWAYS love and support you no matter what you do.*
- *Never apologize for being who you are.*
- *Be a girl with mind, a woman with an attitude and a lady with class.*
- *Never tear down another woman, especially based on what you see on the outside because you have no idea what battles she may be fighting or what barriers she had to overcome to get where she is.*
- *You are strong, powerful and beautiful no matter what your outward package might look like.*
- *"Whether you think you can or think you can't-you're right." (Henry Ford)*
- *Your mind is a garden; your thoughts are the seeds. You can grow flowers or you can grow weeds.*
- *God's got this and God's got you which means you got this too!*

Here are some scriptures that will help you along in your journey:

Deuteronomy 31:6 (NIV) - Be strong and courageous. Do not be afraid or terrified because of them, or the LORD your God goes with you; he will never leave you nor forsake you.

Phillipians 4:13 (NIV) - I can do all things through him who strengthens me.

Proverbs 3:5-6 (NIV) - Trust in the LORD with all your heart, and do not lean on your own understanding. In all your ways acknowledge him, and he will make straight your paths.

Romans 8:28 (NIV) - And we know that in all things God works for the good of those who love him, who have been called according to his purpose.

We pray every word in this book helps to inspire, be a source of strength, comfort and encouragement; may these words be something you can look upon in the time of need. Continue to shine and be great!

Love Always…All the Black Moms

Made in the USA
Monee, IL
02 August 2021